"HOW TO CATCH THEM" SERIES

This is the most famous and best-selling series of books on angling ever published. They have been praised and recommended by *The Angling Times*, *The Field*, *Angling*, *Trout and Salmon*, *The Journal of the Flyfishers' Club*, *The Fishing Gazette*, *A.C.A. Quarterly Review*, *The Midland Angler*, *Angler's World*, *Gamekeeper and Countryside*, *The Fishing Tackle Dealer* and *Angler's Annual*.

The How To Catch Them books are edited by Kenneth Mansfield.

(continued overleaf)

SEA TROUT
HOW TO CATCH THEM

By
F. W. HOLIDAY

LONDON: HERBERT JENKINS

First published by
Herbert Jenkins Limited
2, Clement's Inn
London W.C.2
1956

Second Printing 1961
Third Printing 1967

MADE AND PRINTED IN GREAT BRITAIN
BY D. R. HILLMAN & SONS LTD., FROME

CONTENTS

PREFACE

FEW fish in British waters have been at once the source of so much keen pleasure and so much disappointment as the sea trout. There are anglers who have spent time and money, travelling hundreds of miles, only to return home without a single fish. There are others—perhaps snatching a brief week-end excursion—who have returned to their friends with glowing eyes to tell of sea trout adventures which they will remember for the rest of their lives.

Sea trout are possibly the most difficult fish to catch by sporting methods to be found in Britain. They are ultra-sensitive to vibration, have keen vision, and seem to be capable of learning. Any experienced angler who has pricked a sea trout knows that it is useless to try for the same fish for a long time. Anything at all suspicious in the presentation of fly or bait is detected at once. If fish can be called intelligent then I should rate the sea trout highly.

Sea trout fishing is not a sort of inferior salmon fishing. Many anglers who could fish for salmon if they wished prefer to catch sea trout. However it must be warmly conceded that sea trout fishing is generally much cheaper than salmon fishing, both in respect of licence fees and of tackle. This of course is all to the good. Holiday sea trout fishing is well within the means of most coarse-fish anglers, and this small book shows how to set about it.

The successful sea trouter is usually a lone

bird. As he steps silently along the river bank at dusk, dressed in dark clothing, he becomes almost as much a denizen of the countryside as the owl or the otter. More than one roach angler has turned his patience and concentration to good account when angling for sea trout. A man skilled in casting a fly will often spoil his chance of a fish by moving about restlessly. A less expert performer will basket a couple of fine fish simply because he knew how to keep still. Lack of skill may be overcome; lack of care is almost always the background to failure.

The sea trout is a poem of nature—wild, beautiful and as free as any living creature can be. His fair capture by rod and line is a fascinating pursuit in which I hope increasing numbers of anglers will share.

> *Down amongst the gravels lie,*
> *Wise beyond skill of worm or fly,*
> *This sea trout be the boss of I.*

SOME SPECIMEN SEA TROUT

THE largest sea trout appear to come from continental rivers, from which exceptional fish of between 30 and 40 lb. have been recorded. In Britain, most double-figure sea trout come from a comparatively small list of rivers. From a study of the evidence it seems clear that these big fish are members of localized races which are in the habit of journeying far out to sea where the feeding is particularly good. Rivers from which specimen sea trout have been recorded are the Tweed, Ailort, Ythan, Dovey, Conway and Frome. Anglers should bear in mind however that sea trout sometimes return to rivers other than the ones in which they were hatched. A big sea trout therefore may turn up in any river.

WEIGHT	CAPTOR	PLACE	SEASON
22½ lb.	- S. R. Dwight	- R. Frome	- 1946
	(British Record Sea Trout)		
21 lb.	- Hardy-Corfe	- R. Frome	- 1918
21½ lb.	- C. F. P. Lowe	- R. Conway	- 1955
	(Welsh Record Sea Trout)		
20 lb. 2 oz.	T. Williams	- R. Dovey	- 1936
21 lb.	- Rev. Upcher	- R. Awe	- 1908
	(Scottish Record Sea Trout)		

Large numbers of fine sea trout of between 10 and 15 lb. are netted each season in many river estuaries. In many cases they are mistaken for salmon and are not given the credit due to them. Sometimes anglers make the same error. It is at least possible therefore that big sea trout have a wider distribution than the figures suggest.

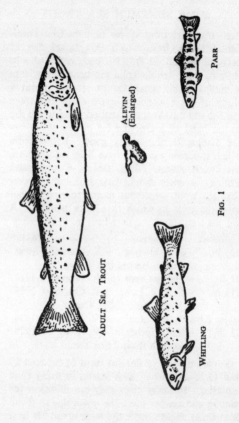

ADULT SEA TROUT

ALEVIN
(Enlarged)

PARR

WHITLING

Fig. 1

10

CHAPTER I

ALTERNATIVE NAMES

SEA TROUT have a variety of local names, and the angler who is unfamiliar with them is apt to become confused when seeking information from country folk. In Wales they are known as sewin. In Scotland young sea trout are called whitling or finnock. In Ireland the identical fish is known as a white trout. Herling, black-nebs, peal, redfins and Lammasmen are other names in use. The angler unfamiliar with sea trout is often confused further by the fact that two names may be in simultaneous use on the same river. A fisherman may tell you that he has just been broken by a lovely sea trout but not to worry as he has a couple of nice herling in the bag. He means that he has lost an adult fish but is fortunate enough to have landed two that are not quite mature. On the other hand " sewin " is a term often used to describe any and every stage of sea trout, from smolts to big fish.

WHAT IS A SEA TROUT ?

Many sea trout anglers ask themselves this question, especially when they see a fish that has spent a long time in fresh water. For the sea trout soon loses its silver coat and becomes dark; so dark that it may easily be mistaken for a brown trout. " There are plenty of ordinary trout in this river," the angler says to himself, " so in

11

what way is the sea trout different since you can sometimes hardly tell them apart?"

The experts are now persuaded that there is only one species of trout—*Salmo trutta*. Therefore the tiny "brownie" living in a foot-wide brook is a blood-relative to the great 20 lb. sea trout leaping the high waterfall. Apart from size, the main difference between them is the migratory instinct.

Why a section of the trout family should have decided to journey to sea is not entirely clear. One very reasonable theory suggests that shortage of natural feed in the river causes the native brown trout to drop downstream to the estuary and sea where they are able to feed richly on marine fare. This is especially plausible since there is a sort of half-and-half stage amongst trout, known as slob trout, which are neither true sea trout nor true brown trout. Moreover, on many small rivers the brown trout normally descend to the lower and deeper reaches during periods of drought. Brown trout which feed in brackish water soon assume a silver coat.

So it seems that a sea trout is simply a sort of trout that migrates to sea because the feeding is richer and more varied than anything it could find in its river haunts. This habit, practised over many thousands of years, is now a compelling instinct.

IDENTIFICATION

Although I said above that sea trout may be confused with brown trout in some circumstances, this event is pretty rare even when the fish have been caught by anglers unfamiliar with the fish. The typical sea trout, fresh from salt water, is a very handsome and distinctive fish. It has a comparatively small head. Its body is deep and firm-fleshed. Its sides are pleasantly ornamented with black spots and its scales glisten like tiny silver coins.

This description refers to a fresh-run fish—" fresh " meaning that it has been in salt water not more than forty-eight hours previously. Identification here presents few difficulties. But sometimes sea trout become isolated in river pools due to sudden drought, or they may be attacked by furunculosis which spoils their prime condition. In such cases even an experienced sea trout angler may hesitate before labelling the fish either " brown trout " or " migratory trout ". Moreover the slob trout further confuse the issue by turning up in the silver garb of true sea trout. With such dubious cases it is best to send a few scales to an expert for microscopic examination and to request his opinion.

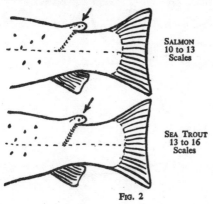

SALMON
10 to 13
Scales

SEA TROUT
13 to 16
Scales

FIG. 2

Very large sea trout are often mistaken for salmon, even by people who should know better. The angler may easily perform a waterside test, however, that clearly establishes whether he has caught a trout or a salmon. The test consists of taking a scale count and in noting the relative positions of maxillary bone to the eye. The scales are counted in an oblique line from the rear end of the adipose fin down to the lateral line. In salmon there will be 10 to 13 scales. In sea trout 13 to 16 (Fig. 2). The maxillary check shows that the sea trout has a larger and longer mouth than a salmon. The rear edge of a trout's mouth extends a little beyond an imaginary line down from the eye, whereas with a salmon the eye and mouth edge are pretty much in line (Fig. 3). I

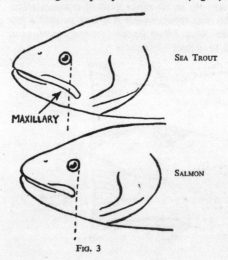

SEA TROUT

MAXILLARY

SALMON

FIG. 3

have always found this test to be quite reliable and now make it as a matter of course on all large fish that I catch.

AGE OF SEA TROUT

Sea trout live longer than salmon and seem to be altogether a more adaptable race. The terrible vitality-drain of spawning causes far less mortality amongst them than it does amongst the salmon clan. Once a sea trout reaches maturity it continues to spawn each year until it dies naturally or is killed. Should it evade the many perils of its wandering life it may reach an age of between twelve and fifteen years. The oldest sea trout known was almost nineteen. But from the angling point of view age is not very important since it bears little relationship to the fish's weight and condition.

FACTORS GOVERNING SIZE

It is plain that some waters produce bigger and fatter sea trout than do others and the names of some of these favoured rivers are noted elsewhere in this book. Since all sea trout spend much of their feeding time in the sea, which is fairly uniform, why is it that the fish vary in size? Surely the sea food supply is not as patchy as all that?

The truth seems to be that sea trout from some rivers are better travellers than their neighbours. Trout from river X may spend much of their time mooching around the coast and estuary. On the other hand the fish from river Z may be used to travelling scores or even hundreds of miles to sea. Mr. W. J. M. Menzies records a young sea trout that was captured 300 miles from the place where it was marked. And when we recall that sea trout usually return to the river where they were born it is easy to see how these large localized races are built up. The inhabitants of most sea trout rivers, however, seem quite satisfied with the more modest off-shore feeding.

SPORTING QUALITIES AND EDIBILITY

Superlatives and warm endorsements of the sea trout's fighting qualities are all very fine, but they tell the would-be sea trouter little of what to expect. Why is the sea trout exceptional as a sporting fish? How does it fight? How long does it fight?

Take a glance at the sketch of a sea trout. Note the perfect streamlining, the thick " wrist " at the tail, and the broad, powerful caudal fin. Remember that this perfectly-designed creature has been in the habit of travelling perhaps hundreds of miles to sea, that it has evaded seals, porpoises, and other predators, and that its nature has made it mount fierce rapids and tumbling waterfalls. Knowing this, we can better understand that a restraint, such as an angler's lure, fixed to its jaw will only serve to unleash some of the driving energy that has served it so well in the past.

A hooked sea trout never surrenders. It uses every trick in the box—and a few more. If sheer speed can give it freedom then it has it. If power is needed then it has that too. If a series of leaps will detach the fly or minnow then it can easily give them. Its stamina is a wonder of nature. Unlike many fish the sea trout never flags or becomes suddenly spent. He fights until all his energy is drained away and, unlike the salmon, seldom sulks on the river bed. This noble fish may be likened to a Spanish fighting bull which charges even while its legs buckle under it.

People who are used to plenty of fresh salmon and sea trout in season are mostly in agreement that fresh sea trout provides the finer dish of the two. Prime sea trout flesh is pink, slightly oily, and has a deliciously rich flavour that few people can resist.

CHAPTER II

LIFE AND MIGRATION

DEVELOPMENT OF THE SEA TROUT

THE biological study of the sea trout's life story is an intricate business to which specialists have devoted lifetimes. Every angler who hopes to catch sea trout should know at least the rudiments of this story. By knowing "Why" he will be in a better position to determine "When" and "Where" when it comes to fishing.

The hen sea trout lays her eggs in the river gravels, where they are fertilized by the cock fish. The spot where the eggs are laid, fertilized, and covered with a mound of gravel is called a redd. In the tiny tributaries of sea trout rivers these humps of stones and grit are a common sight. Sometimes the redd is left high and dry when the flood water recedes and the eggs, of course, perish. The eggs in the redds are often devoured by trout, waterside birds, or even by sea trout. Quite often other sea trout try to make their redds on top of the original and, in doing so, damage or expose the first batch of eggs. This is known as over-cutting and on some rivers it presents the keepers with a difficult problem.

The eggs in an undisturbed redd hatch out in about three months, the actual time depending on the water temperature. The baby sea trout, which now looks at the world for the first time, is in a fortunate position. It carries its own food supply around with it in the form of a bag under

its tummy. This little creature, known as an
alevin, spends the next six weeks or so lying
under stones out of the way of hungry trout. At
the end of that time it is ready to cruise around a
little and investigate its strange new world, It
obeys its instinct enough to dart to cover when a
shadow crosses the stream and so avoids the
thrusting bill of many a kingfisher. The young
fish grows slowly and takes on the distinctive
" stripes " which is the royal insignia of all young
trout and salmon. It is then termed a parr.

After roughly two years in the river as a parr
the young sea trout feels some magical call within
its cells that tells it that its baby days are over.
Dropping farther and farther downstream it
meets with others of its kind and the little fish
form shoals. It is now called a smolt and it has
taken on a bright silvery sheen. These smolts
gather in thousands in some deep pool a mile or
two above tidal influence. They play and dodge
and dart about like kids in a nursery. The season
for this is usually early May. Then, one night
when the tide rolls in, the fish go out with it.
Like parties of children leaving school they have
trooped away into the great world of ocean.

In the salt waters of the estuary the smolts find
food such as they have never known before. The
oily copepods exist in millions just waiting to be
eaten. There are young sand eels, the larvae of
various types of shellfish, shrimps and prawns,
and succulent little fish such as sparling. The
list of marine fare is as lengthy as it is nourishing.

The young sea trout is now known as a whitling,
or by some of the alternative names mentioned in
the first chapter. In the company of a shoal it

may venture for some distance out to sea. Marked whitling have been captured as much as fifty miles offshore.

The whitling comes back to its native river after its first sea journey in the late summer or autumn, and it is not very much larger than when it left. It may weigh anything between 4 oz. and 1 lb. What it does then is problematic. It may loaf around in the estuary, or it may go for a cruise into the river's middle reaches. As the year wears on, however, large numbers of whitling, now grown to about $\frac{1}{2}$ lb. or more in weight, will advance up the river. Many anglers must have been stirred, the way I have been stirred, by the sight of these small silvery fish leaping time and again at some great fall. The leap of a salmon is majestic. But the spry leap of a whitling is enough to move even the most unimaginative spectator. Nothing can daunt the young sea trout. His names are courage, determination, and persistence.

At this stage in its life the sea trout is quite unpredictable. Even the biologists admit that they are often baffled. Some of the whitling's generation may be at sea. Others may be sporting in the estuary or in the river's lower reaches. Others again may have run up to the headwaters of the river, either to change their minds and return, or else to actually form redds, spawn and behave altogether like adult fish. This is what makes the sea trout's history so absorbing. The fish are not robots but seem to show individuality. The whitling sea trout is a restless little chap, not yet sure whether to behave like a boy or a man.

The following spring the whitling return once

more to the sea, whether they have spawned or not, and as they begin to feed and develop they are known as one-winter sea trout. Journeying to sea in search of food the sea trout now grow quickly and that summer return to their native river as fat fish of between 1½ and 2 lb. in weight. That autumn most of them will spawn and the following spring will see them dropping back once more to the sea. This is the cycle round which the rest of their lives revolve.

WHEN DO SEA TROUT RUN ?

The sea trout angler should have a good working knowledge of the fish's migration times if he is to enjoy sport. Otherwise, obviously, he may find himself on parts of the river that are empty of fish. A few minutes spent thinking the matter over may, quite literally, save hours of frustration and disappointment, not to say expense.

The main run of sea trout in most rivers is from midsummer onwards. Let me state this rather more clearly. If you intend taking a holiday sea trout fishing it is unwise to select May or early June. Late June, July or August are preferable. With such a varying factor as the habits of fish, though, one cannot be dogmatic. A very wet May might well bring up a run of fish in the early June days. A summer drought can postpone the sea trout migration until the autumn. The mean height of the river is of the greatest importance. Therefore check the season against the prevailing weather before setting forth on a long journey after sea trout. A year of normal rainfall will see nice shoals of fish in the river by mid-June and sport may be expected until the season closes. Generally speaking, the more rain—short of violent floods—the more fish. Sea trout love a full, dark river.

EARLY RIVERS

A word now about early rivers for sea trout. Although the main runs of fish enter the stream about midsummer, there are sometimes early arrivals. I am not speaking now of whitling, which may be playing around in the estuary in March or April, but of adult fish.

The biologists seem uncertain about whether there is a true run of spring sea trout in some rivers or whether these fish are simply impatient forerunners of the summer migration. The fact remains, however, that big sea trout sometimes do forge their way into the river in the early months. These fish often weigh between 5 and 15 lb.—sometimes even larger. They are a particular challenge to the angler since luring them is difficult and landing them even more so. Several years of age has given these fish a great cunning in rushing and smashing their way to freedom. I know one river where several anglers are broken up each spring by what are sometimes called " grilse ". In fact the fish are big spring sea trout which frequent this river in some numbers.

SEA TROUT RUNS AND THE WEATHER

I mentioned the weather in an earlier paragraph, but the subject is of such basic importance it seems wise to expand the thing into particulars. The beginner who arrives laden with hope and

tackle may well ask the landlord of his hotel:
" What is good sea trout weather?"—and that
worthy will be stumped for an answer. The
landlord may ask the angler: " Do you mean
good weather for the fish to run, good weather
to catch them by fly at night, by spinning during
the day—or what?" If the angler is not sure of
what he means the conversation is fated to become a talk on sea trout and the weather delivered
by the experienced host. To save the busy man
his trouble I offer a few pointers here.

Sea trout can be caught during periods of high
or low water, by day or by night, provided the
right approach is made and provided the fish are
in the river. Both these provisos are determined
by the weather.

Let us take an imaginary fishing season. The
May is a dry month with only a few light showers
that have no effect on river level. June comes in
equally dry, but in the second week a succession
of thunderstorms turns the river, for a few days,
into a boiling cocoa flood. Mid-June sees a
return of warm, settled weather. Are conditions
good for fishing? They couldn't be better! The
rain has filled the river with fish and the creels
should soon be weighty.

Take another season. Cold, unsettled weather
has ushered in another British " summer ". May
is a miserable wet month. June is even worse
and the hotel-keepers are wishing they ran duck
farms. How of the river? It is certainly at a
nice level but it is unlikely to yield much to the
rods until it falls. The fish have come up all
right but the constant high water unsettles them.
Moreover, the continuing cold is against good

baskets. Although local anglers can still take a nice brace of sea trout from certain select spots we should be well advised to postpone our trip, if possible, until the water drops and warms a little.

As for local conditions at the time of going fishing I myself have no particular preference except that it should be reasonably warm. I have taken sea trout during thunder rain as well as in the dusk of a torrid July day. The state of the river is much more important than the local state of the atmosphere. A badly droughted river, of course, is hopeless.

CHAPTER III

IN GENERAL

THE sea trout is the natural denizen of every
briskly flowing stream in Britain. The fact that
it is not found in every stream is an appalling
monument to man's ruthless lack of concern for
everything except material wealth. Instead of being
restricted to certain parts of the country the sea
trout should disport itself in every beck and
brook. It did so once; and it may do so again.
But, alas, the day is distant. The sea trout's
needs are simple; it asks only for clean flowing
water and gravel beds in which to spawn. But
in our atom age these common things are depress-
ingly rare. Thus the sea trout has retreated to
the less industrialized portions of the island, and
it is there we must seek him.

With so vigorous and travelled a fish as the
sea trout it is not surprising to find that its distribution is very wide. The British Isles are only
a small portion of its range. It is found from
Cornwall to the Scottish Isles and over to the
west coast of Ireland. South of the border it is
confined to rivers running to the western and
southern seaboard, although there is now a good
chance that it will colonize other rivers as I shall
mention presently.

WHAT TO PAY

Before talking about where to fish, in detail, it

may be a good idea to deal now with the question of charges. Many anglers still feel that sea trout fishing must be a game for the wealthy sportsman. There is a general impression that unless one stays at an hotel, hires a professional assistant, and pays quite a lot of money, there is no sea trout fishing to be had. This is a legend without substance.

I would like to make another point here. Game fishing at one time had a sort of snob value. In Britain—but not in America—it became the preserve of the well-to-do. To read the literature of that period one gathers that fly-fishing and game fish must have been created for one certain section of the population. Fortunately much of this nonsense has disappeared. The sea trout is as likely to fall victim to a minnow thrown by a labourer as it is to a coloured trifle cast by a learned barrister. Nowadays the angler who takes the record sea trout of the season from some well-known river probably turns out to be a factory worker from the nearest industrial belt. Sea trout fishing—and, surely, all fishing— is and ought to be the privilege of every citizen willing to go in search of it.

" What will it cost?" is a question everyone must ask. There is little use in advising someone where to go sea trout fishing if they are worrying in advance over the bill. How much for a week's holiday? How about licences?

In England and Wales the sea trout angler's first necessity is a River Board licence for Migratory Trout. These licences may be taken out to cover a season, a fortnight and, in some cases, a week. The cost, of course, is proportionately reduced.

Although the charge varies between the different River Boards, the average charge, for a week, is about £1. In some cases it may be 30s., although some Boards charge as little as 7s. 6d. The River Board licence can be bought after you arrive at your selected river area. They are stocked by most tackle-dealers. When the licence becomes invalid and you return home, do remember to fill in the " Return of Fish Caught " on the back and send it to the Fishery Officer whose address is printed at the top. These officials rely on the angler's co-operation in this matter and the information gained about weight and size of fish is valuable for assessing the worth of different waters.

Now about fees. There need be nothing breathtaking in this. In fact a lengthy list could be compiled of sea trout fishing that is quite free. In England and Wales there is no charge for fishing in the tidal water of estuaries although a River Board licence, of course, is required.

The angler, however, should take care not to trespass on private property in order to reach the fishing. In Scotland a different law applies and estuary fishing is often rented or leased. South of the border there is a huge amount of brackish water fishing for which you need not pay a penny. I will have more to say later about the quality of estuary fishing for sea trout.

What does it cost to fish in one of the well-known sea trout rivers? To this question the only answer is: It depends in which part of the river you want to fish. There are very few completely private rivers in Britain to-day. Even the most famous waters have lengths and stretches controlled by clubs, angling associations, and other bodies. These are usually glad to issue visitors with temporary fishing tickets. The fee for this privilege will range from 5s. to £1 for the week, or perhaps £2 or £3 if the water is especially noted. The angler who is more concerned with quality than expense may find the private waters of a good hotel more to his taste. If he is determined to go the whole hog and get the best fishing possible, perhaps sharing the expense with a couple of angling friends, he would do best to contact a reputable tacklist in the area of his choice. He will soon be put in touch with owners who have private river-beats for rent.

WHICH RIVER ?

The sea trout, to-day, is mainly a fish of the west and north. If the angler prefers to travel as little as possible to reach the fishing then his choice must fall within certain groups. London anglers will be attracted by the south-west and will consider the merits of the Frome, Exe, Teign, Tamar, Torridge or Taw. From London north to the Midlands anglers should certainly investigate the claims of Welsh sea trout rivers before going farther afield. Notable ones are the Towy, Teifi, Rheidol, Dovey, Glaslyn and Conway. The angler fishing in Scotland has an excellent variety of sea trout waters to choose from, lochs as well as rivers. The Tweed, the Spey and the Ailort are outstanding for sea trout and the fish run very big. Lesser waters are too numerous to list. Many waters, such as the Ythan, fish particularly well in the tidal portion.

Some of the rivers listed above are famous and

much sought after and the fishing is expensive but the angler of moderate means should not feel discouraged. There are hundreds of small rivers holding sea trout where the sport is sometimes very good. Get a large-scale map of the area you hope to visit and study it.

SEA TROUT IN EASTERN ENGLAND

Sea trout have been driven from rivers in eastern England by a combination of pollution, water-abstraction and silting-up. Yet these hardy, adaptable fish are constantly trying to re-colonize their old-time haunts. A migration takes place each season into the North Sea by sea trout from Northumberland. Many of these fish wander southwards feeding on shoals of young herrings. Some of them try to ascend rivers in Yorkshire and East Anglia and specimens have been taken on the Norfolk Broads and in Suffolk. I myself once saw a sea trout of about 5 lb. trying to swim up a tidal channel near Felixstowe.

With a little encouragement sea trout will return once more to the east and there are signs that this encouragement is being offered. Within a few years many rivers may once more welcome back this unique migratory fish. In 1951 a sea trout of over 9 lb. was taken from Dedham mill-pool on the Suffolk Stour and the local angling clubs there have seen several smaller fish. At the time of writing this river is being planted with salmon ova. Should a run develop no doubt sea trout ova will be tried also.

Another river with an immediate sea trout future is the Kentish Stour. The Kent River Board is trying, by the introduction of ova, to re-establish the runs of sea trout which were a feature of this stream many years ago.

MOORLAND TYPE STREAMS

Although sea trout will run up sluggish waterways they seem to be more at home in rapid streams of the sort that tumble down from moorlands. In fact the faster and rockier the stream the better the run of sea trout. In these moorland streams the brown trout are usually quite small. There is a theory that the sea trout evolved from these freshwater trout and learned its migratory habit because the food supply in the river was deficient. There is certainly much to be said for this because slow, alkali streams, rich in fly-life, hold few sea trout, although the brown trout thrive. It is the barren, acid rivers that the sea trout seems to favour, the rivers of so-called " hard " water.

LOCATING SEA TROUT IN RIVERS

Fig. 4 gives an approximate idea of how sea trout may expect to be distributed in a typical moorland river in differing months of the season. One assumes that it is a season of moderate rainfall.

Fishing in April and May is best practised in the lower reaches, not overlooking the estuary. Small sea trout—whitling—of ¾lb. and upwards may be taken on fly or minnow. I know some anglers object to the practice of killing whitling but, for myself, I can see little harm in taking a couple of the fish if nothing better offers. In any case I do not think rod-fishing—as distinct from netting—affects the number of migratory fish in a

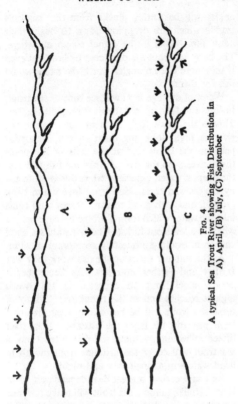

FIG. 4
A typical Sea Trout River showing Fish Distribution in
A) April, (B) July, (C) September

river very much. Huge numbers of young sea
trout are hatched and huge numbers must disappear at sea for a variety of reasons. The
sportsman, I feel, can affect the balance very
little. By the end of May, sometimes earlier, the

angler will be getting plucks from that season's smolts which are dropping down to begin their adult life. This is the signal to go elsewhere. The baby sea trout are protected by law; but even if they were not no angler worth the name would fish for them.

Water of average level will see runs of sea trout, in June and July, up into the river's middle reaches. This is the place to seek them out. When the river is high, look for them in the deep runs between the pools and at the tails of the pools themselves. As the river shrinks the fish will find the deepest water, especially when this is protected by bushes and trees. Sea trout love dense bank growth, and with good reason. Trees send roots into the water which form a protective cage behind which the sea trout lurks. There it stands a good chance of evading a questing cormorant or otter.

As the summer wears on the fish work their way farther and farther up-river. By September a goodly stock may be expected in the river's highest reaches and in the tributaries. Many of these sea trout will be beautifully fresh fish that have just run up from the estuary. In a river fifteen miles long, without serious obstructions, a sea trout will cover the distance from mouth to head waters in a single day and night.

As I said earlier, a great deal depends on water level. Unlike salmon, sea trout will make progress upstream even when the water is quite low. But they travel best when the water is at, or above, average height. To find sea trout in the river, study the height and condition of the water in relation to the season.

CHAPTER IV

FLY-FISHING FOR SEA TROUT

IN GENERAL

ALTHOUGH I am certainly not a "fly only" purist,
I think, nevertheless, that fly-fishing is the most
satisfying method of angling for these fish. Even
more to the point it is a very killing method, and
in this book we are especially concerned with how
to catch sea trout. The would-be sea trouter is
therefore urged to study "the fly" from the
point of view that it is a most effective way of
getting a few of those fat silvery fish on to the
grass. We have already been told *ad nauseum*
how sporting fly-fishing is, so will take it as read.
In my belief the competent fly-fisher stands a
better chance of coming away with his creel
loaded than does the angler who practices other
fishing methods. I speak, of course, of the expert.
But do not overlook the point that all experts
were once beginners.

TACKLE

The tackle for fly-fishing for sea trout need not
be expensive but it must be suitable. A friend of
mine picked up an excellent fly-rod at a jumble
sale for ten shillings. A coat of varnish and a
set of new rings put it in the fifteen guinea class.
Weight and length are the two points to watch
with rods. The weight—assuming a split-cane rod
—should be between about 5 and 8 oz. A 6-oz.
rod is admirable and has enough backbone to

handle a big fish. The length should be between 8 and 9½ feet. I speak here of rods suitable for smallish rivers in which 90 per cent of sea trouting is done. Rod material is a matter of taste. Having tried glass and metal rods, I have now returned to my old love—split-cane, but, as I say, it is a matter of opinion.

Reels for the game are of the normal fly-reel type. The main thing to note when buying a fly-reel is to ensure that it, and the fly-line, balance the rod. In fact rod, reel and line should be assembled at the tacklist's and the outfit carefully checked. The place normally gripped by the hand, above the reel seating, should find there a point of balance. By trying larger, then smaller, reels you soon find one that suits the rod. An ill-balanced outfit is awkward to use and may well prejudice the angler against fly-fishing altogether as being too hard for him to learn.

Fly-lines are of numerous types. All are heavy to facilitate casting. Some are tapered or have a "torpedo head" and are not cheap to buy. While tapered lines are an undoubted asset for dry-fly fishing, I consider that a level line is quite suitable for wet-fly fishing for sea trout, especially at night. And level lines are much cheaper. I would rather use a sound level line costing, say, 10s., than use an ancient tapered line because I could not afford £3 for a new one.

As regards casts, I plump for nylon monofilament in assorted thicknesses to suit varying conditions. Monofil is cheap—and therefore may be renewed frequently; it is reliable, and it does not need soaking before use. Moreover, I like the springiness of monofilament. This acts as a useful shock-absorber when playing a difficult fish.

The other essentials of the fly-fisher's outfit may be left to taste. A landing-net with a long handle is useful, but not essential. Personally I prefer a telescopic trout-size gaff. It may be carried in the bag or creel and will be more effective if you hook a double-figure fish than would a too-small net. Small sea trout can be run aground on a sand-bar, and big ones too sometimes.

FLIES

The colourful legions that march across the tacklist's counter are enough to give us all nightmares of indecision for a month, especially if we are not too sure of what the fish like. And what angler truthfully is sure? Most people blindly take pot-luck and what they can afford. In the circumstances perhaps this is the wisest course.

To be bold about it, however, we will pick six flies—two for night use and four for day. The night flies are: Teal-and-Silver and Connemara Black. The day flies are: Peter Ross, Mallard-and-Claret, Alexandra and Invicta. These, of course, are all wet flies, for fishing below the water surface. I suggest that they should be dressed to size 8 hooks for all normal work. But for low water fishing, or for when there is strong sunlight, a few flies as small as size 4 should be carried. These few patterns represent my choice. But if I had left my flies at home and had to borrow one at the river-side I should request, if possible, a Teal-and-Silver. If the fish were moving at all I think I might get one with this pattern.

FLY-FISHING BY DAY

Many anglers wonder if it is necessary to wade in order to fly-fish for sea trout. It depends on the river. Never wade unless you have to, in order to cover the fish, and then do so as gingerly and slowly as possible. The angler who sloshes about in the water is wasting his time if he hopes to catch sea trout. Never wade if you can walk. A sea trout can detect water-vibrations up to, I fancy, fifty yards. It has to do. If an otter gets in the pool its life may depend on knowing the fact at once.

Some sea trout anglers tie a number of flies to their cast. I use only two. One, tied at the end of the cast, which is known as the tail-fly, and a second, tied some two feet up the cast to a short piece of monofilament, which is called the dropper. Many successful anglers use only one fly and, for night fishing, one fly is certainly enough to manage.

Having got the rod set up, the line threaded, and the flies on the cast, we are ready to start operations. Standing near the tail of a run with the current sweeping down and fanning out below us into a pool it is obviously going to be best to cast across and upstream. The current will seize line and flies and swing them down and round into deep water. Any fish lying facing upstream will thus have a broadside view of the flies moving across its field of vision, which is what we want.

While the flies are in the current they will have plenty of life and movement. Once they reach the quieter waters of the pool however we must use our judgment on whether to impart movement to the flies or not, by working the rod-tip. I like to work the flies gently and spasmodically, imagining that they are tiny fish butting across the water. Once the flies lie directly downstream from the angler they should be slowly recovered ready for the next cast.

In Fig. 5 I show where sea trout are likely to

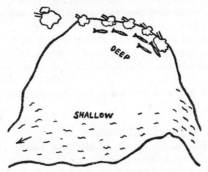

Position of Sea Trout in pool by day

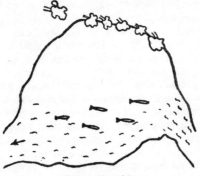

Same pool at night

FIG. 5

lie in a typical pool by day, assuming the water to be of average height. It is therefore good tactics to get your flies under the cover of trees whenever possible, and sink them well. If you can cast directly under the trees—good. If not, cast above and let the current do the rest. In still water slow deep fishing usually gives the best results.

Some anglers favour the use of a fly garnished with a maggot. The method is often very killing after a little rain and should be tried. The maggot should be mounted very carefully since the attraction of this method lies in the lively movement of the bait.

FLY-FISHING BY NIGHT

This is the aspect of sea trout fishing that makes men leave their wives and live in hotels with no other company than a fishing-rod. What is its magic? What the secret? I do not know. A hundred fishing books have failed to lay bare the mystery.

Night fly-fishing must be carefully planned, else all is disaster. Mount half a dozen night flies on as many casts and wrap each one on a separate strip of cardboard with the attachment loops nipped into slots. Take two torches with you as one alone is guaranteed to fall into the water. Refreshment, liquid or otherwise, and a capacious landing-net complete the night fisher's outfit. I might add that it is preferable, unless you are very strong and silent, to fish with a companion. This is for the lending of aid to deal with possible big fish quite as much as for the lending of moral support during the witching hours.

It has always seemed a fascinating mystery to me how sea trout can sense a fly at night. The solution is probably that summer nights are never really dark. A fish looking upwards no doubt sees much activity amongst surface insects by virtue of their silhouettes. Quite possibly some fly dressings have a fluorescent effect. Whatever the case, the flies are distinctly sensed and are taken with a gusto not apparent in daytime.

Casting a fly at night is most difficult if you are determined to throw a long line. Sooner or later the line will hit your rod on the back-cast. Failing that, you will become caught up on vegetation in the rear. This sort of thing happens to almost every angler who goes fly-fishing at night for the first time. It can be avoided by remembering that a short cast is best.

Sea trout cruise close inshore at night. They splash and feed in the shallows. By casting quite a short line you will reach plenty of fish and will have much less trouble than the chap who insists on trying to throw under the far bank. At night I find that fairly rapid working of the fly gives the best results. Many sea trout are attracted to the fly, no doubt, by the water vibrations.

Some eager anglers hurry to the twilit river and begin fishing just as soon as they can get a fly into the water. A wiser course, I suggest, is to sit on the bank for a few minutes and have a smoke. Assuming that you have chosen a good pool for your night fishing—and by that I mean a deep pool certain to contain fish at that time of the year—it is obvious that some parts of it are better than others. Much can be learned simply by listening to the " plop " of fish rising. The sea trout may be cruising in the current or may be in slack water near the pool's tail. Discover the whereabouts of the fish before making your first cast.

Some anglers like to fish all night, but I confess that my fibre isn't that tough. From ten to twelve on a June night is enough for me. But I am fond of early fishing and have found that from about four o'clock till dawn is often the best time of the whole twenty-four hours. Anglers who camp, like myself, or who can sleep in a car, have a great advantage over their fellows who must catch trains or return to possibly distant hotels.

NOTES ON CASTING

The angler who knows little about fly-fishing is well-advised to put in plenty of practice before trying his luck at night. Casting a fly at night has peculiar problems of its own which must be overcome very soon if the fishing trip is to beget pleasure instead of frustration. There are three main points to watch.

The first is length. In daylight you can see exactly where your line and flies are going. At night, there is only the sense of touch to guide you. Find out what is the minimum amount of line that it takes to make your rod " work " properly. It will probably be about four yards. I suggest that no cast should be longer than this, at least not until you are fairly confident. Attempts to cast a long line at night, without much experience, invariably end in trouble. And there is no need for lengthy casting because the sea trout are often only a few yards away.

The second point is the back-cast. On the

back-cast, the line and rod must move backwards
on two slightly different planes otherwise, of
course, the line will hit the rod. In daytime
most anglers seem to judge the amount instinct-
ively. But not always at night. Last season an
experienced trout-fishing friend of mine broke the
tip of his rod when his line fouled it during a
back-cast. The best way to avoid the trouble is
to slightly exaggerate your rod movements, allowing plenty for line clearance (Fig. 6).

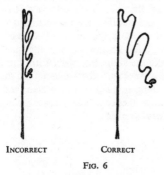

INCORRECT   CORRECT

FIG. 6

Back-cast viewed from rear. At night
enough clearance must be allowed

Physical snags, such as bushes, are a menace to
most would-be night anglers. They get caught up
repeatedly and their outing degenerates into a
hunt amongst adjectival undergrowth to free line
and fly. So I say—pick your pool. Make sure
you have plenty of casting distance, both fore and
aft. And if you can get someone to teach you,
try to learn the Switch cast.

WATER CONDITIONS

The night angler needs warm, medium to low water for his fly-fishing operations. I have never found night fly-fishing much good after heavy rain nor when the night was close and thundery. A spell of settled weather is necessary both for personal comfort and for finding fish willing to take.

Much has been said about lunar and tidal influences on this branch of fishing. I do not know whether the tide affects river fish—I doubt it, but I feel that the moon certainly does. At least it appears to affect the weather, and this in turn makes or mars the sport. I dislike a full moon shining full on the water in the same way that I dislike the sun. But apart from this I am quite willing to take what comes. If the sea trout are willing to take they will take, and it is doubtful if any theory will ever cover the various subtle factors involved.

CHAPTER V

ABOUT SPINNING

"SPINNING" and "Threadlining" are now synonymous terms amongst thousands of anglers, and with good reason. Baits may now be cast with next to no effort. Hard-wearing monofilament lines are everywhere available. A wide assortment of excellent reels are in the tacklist's window. Spinning is now threadlining, and vice versa. The track uncovered by the late Mr. Alexander Wanless has now become a highway along which thousands of happy anglers pass each season.

I therefore propose to ignore the centre-pin reel in this section, although this type of reel has its special uses in drop-minnowing, prawning, and other methods to be described later.

Spinning is an admirable way of catching sea trout if suitable tackle is used. It is both sporting and interesting. At certain times it is deadly. For long spells it is useless. Sometimes the fish will throw themselves at a bait in order to seize it. On other occasions they will parade behind it in a disgusted shoal as though commenting to each other on the crudeness of the artifice.

Many anglers rely entirely on spinning to provide their sport with sea trout since these migratory fish are avid seizers of moving objects. Yet I have noticed, amongst such anglers, very often, a sort of stereotyped approach to their art.

For instance, some people use devon minnows and never vary their tactics from the start of the season to the close. They throw their lures over the water with no clear idea of where the fish are lying. One pool is treated exactly like another. Many spend half their time fishing water that cannot hold sea trout, by the very nature of the fish. Light intensity and water level are two other factors ignored or improperly understood. All this leads to lost opportunities. Unimaginative tactics take few sea trout.

SPINNING TACKLE

The outfit for threadline spinning for sea trout has now standardized itself to a 7-ft. rod, a small threadline reel and a monofilament line of 4 lb. breaking strain. This is the basic outfit, and the angler who chooses to vary it should do so reluctantly, for its efficiency and aptness for the job are demonstrated a thousand times each season.

I have tried glass and metal rods, but always seem to go back to split cane, which is friendly stuff to handle and of known staunchness when it comes to a test. A 7-ft. rod is better than one longer or shorter simply because this length seems to be ideal for imparting the essential " flick " to a small bait. The weight for a tool of this sort should be around 4 oz.

Threadline reels have also standardized themselves. In addition to ratchet-checked spools they now have optional anti-reverse levers and full-hoop pick-up arms. The sea trout angler will have no trouble in finding one to suit his pocket and his taste, but it should be a small reel, the smaller and neater the better. If the cash runs to it he should certainly buy a spare spool, unless a spare is provided. This will allow two thicknesses of line to be available according to the water conditions.

Monofilament is the line to use—4-lb. line if the water is medium to high; 2-lb. line if it is low. Many anglers use lines of 10 lb. and upwards for sea trout and the reason, to me, is a complete mystery. The thicker a line becomes the harder it is to cast and the more visible it is to the fish. It seems pointless to use heavy line with a light rod; yet it is often done. One hundred yards of monofil is ample for most rivers. With the larger waterways the outfit should be scaled up to suit. On the Conway for instance I should prefer 150 yards of 5 or 6 lb. line.

Other tackle requirements are a quantity of small black barrel swivels and some large shots to use as anti-kinkers. I do not like the celluloid gadgets sold for this purpose as they gleam like mirrors in oblique light. The ball-bearing swivels on the market are excellent for heavy spinning but are too large for sea trout in medium water.

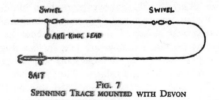

FIG. 7
SPINNING TRACE MOUNTED WITH DEVON

THE NATURAL MINNOW

As a spinning—or a wobbling—bait for sea trout I unhesitatingly choose the natural minnow before anything else. Fig. 8 shows minnow tackles with and without bait. Both tackles and minnows may be had from any good stockist.

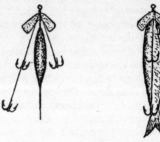

FIG. 8
NATURAL MINNOW TACKLE

There are some who catch their minnows in traps and go through a lengthy process of preserving them for future use. A few anglers like to catch their minnows at the river-bank for use the same day. None of this is necessary unless you enjoy messing about more than fishing. Minnows may now be had in packets, toughened and sweetly preserved, at a price of about 1s. a dozen; 1½-2-in. minnows are best for sea trout. A two-dozen packet of these baits will see you through a long day's fishing. They kill quite as well as fresh minnows, I find, and stay on the tackle much better. The minnow packet is best emptied into a linen bag full of salt. Unused minnows will last for a month in this, if necessary, if kept dry.

ARTIFICIALS

Most artificial spinning baits are attractive to sea trout, and the fish can be caught on phantoms, quill-minnows, devons, spoons, and small plugs. My own choice of artificial bait is the quill-minnow, and these I make in batches during the winter. Fig. 9 shows a quill-minnow and the component parts thereof. A few goose or swan quills, a quantity of size 12 treble hooks, swivels, some 10 lb. wire and a reel of tying silk are the raw materials. By making your own you save half a crown on each bait and get a lot of fun during the dark evenings. Sea trout will take a quill readily.

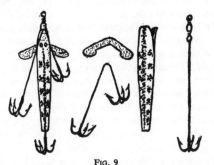

FIG. 9
QUILL MINNOW SHOWING COMPONENTS

The metal type of artificial comes into its own when the water is dark after a spate. In such conditions there is no substitute for a silver devon of about 1½ inches in length. Some anglers fancy mixed colours—silver-and-blue, silver-and-gold, or other variations. Much depends on the relative darkness of sky and water on what size and colour of devon to use. A useful test is to spin the bait in about two feet of water. If it is easily seen then tend to use a smaller size (down to ¾ in. if necessary) and darker colours. If the water is dingy and the bait scarcely visible then use larger size devons with plenty of silver on them. The fish should be able to see the bait from a distance of about 3–4 feet. On the other hand, if you send a large devon flashing through clear water they will be startled. Experiment and a little experience soon guide the spinning-angler on to the right path.

I am also very fond of using a small spoon— say 1 in.—when both day and water are dark. Small spoons take sea trout well when fished in the back waters of spated rivers. The treble hooks of such spoons should be attached to a length of monofilament or to a leaded rod, never to the spoon itself. The reason is that a sea trout goes almost mad when hooked and if given the chance will lever a treble free in a twinkling. This is an additional reason for my liking for quill minnows, which have trebles attached to short lengths of monofilament or gut. The same argument applies to metal devons; always use the patterns that run up the trace when a fish is hooked. I lost a lot of fish before I made this a regular drill. (Fig. 10.)

SPINNING IN HIGH WATER

When a spell of wet weather fills the summer river from bank to bank, then the spinning enthusiast may expect to do his best execution amongst sea trout. If he is staying near the river he will go down to the water frequently and eye the flood with anxious eyes. But all is well; the river is still rising. The time to get cracking is when it starts to fall. The first sympton of this is a lightening in the colour of the water. From brown or yellow the tint changes through various shades of amber to a lovely honey-colour. By then rod, line and bait should be ready and the angler about his business.

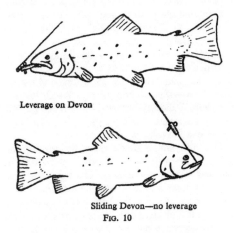

Leverage on Devon

Sliding Devon—no leverage
Fig. 10

Find a nice run of water, not too rapid, and begin operations by dropping the bait into the slack at the side of the current. Do not be afraid to let the bait fish deep. After a few minutes of this, try the opposite side of the run by casting across and allowing the current to sweep the lure down and round. Recover the bait fairly briskly. Sea trout love a speedy bait. Always keep the rod point as low as possible so

D

that the lure is not drawn to the surface in the middle of the river. Should this happen, any following fish will at once turn away, having detected a sham. On the other hand, if the bait is spun in to one's feet a sea trout will often dart in at the last instant and seize it.

Should these tactics fail it may well be that the river has dropped more than you thought and that the sea trout are now in the pools looking for suitable places to lie and bide a while. Fish the tails and sides of the pools first, casting upstream, straight across, or across and down, as opportunity offers. Cast methodically, once in each place. If a fish plucks at the bait but fails to hook, cast somewhere else for a time and try the place later—after an hour or so. Watch for telltale swirls indicating where fish are moving. Try several sizes and colours of baits until you know which one the fish are willing to nip.

In a river falling after a spate the cream of the fishing is often in the pool above waterfalls or in the first deep water after a long run of rapids. I always make a point of seeking out these places and it does me lots of good. After climbing a difficult fall or struggling up a quarter of a mile of broken water the fish take a rest. And they will usually take a bait. Perhaps they feel like a snack after their exertions.

SPINNING IN LOW WATER

As the river falls to its normal level and becomes colourless, the angler with a spinning-rod must use wily tactics to contact his quarry. The methods I have described above are almost useless in clear water. Indeed many anglers put their spinning rods aside when the river falls to its usual summer level, but I have personally had much sport with sea trout in such conditions and will now describe the ultra-fine spinning methods that did the trick.

One requires a 2 lb. monofilament line and some 1½ in. preserved minnows and tackles to suit. One very small swivel is tied into the trace. Waders are handy and the angler should wear inconspicuous clothing.

It is upstream fishing begun when the sun is off the water—usually about seven o'clock in mid-summer. The places to fish are the throats of the pools and the quiet ripply water flowing alongside steep banks. Beneath trees and bushes is good too —tricky casting but very effective. In low water the sea trout lie close to cover during the daylight hours. Many an angler has glanced at a pool, grumbled about no fish, and walked away while half a dozen beauties lay two yards under his heels. At dusk, sometimes a little earlier, sea trout become active. They yearn to gulp the oxygen in the central current. They become interested in the fish and insect life around them. Moreover, the approach of night keys them up, for that is when the otter does his hunting. The sea trout knows this from thousands of years of inherited instincts.

This sort of fishing yields best results when you are able to cast upstream and slightly across. Fish moving water rather than still. Sea trout will snatch the bait as it slips past or may follow it downstream and take a pull as it turns out of the current. Always aim to show the fish the minnow—not the line and swivel.

The stolid winding favoured by some anglers is quite inappropriate for low water spinning. The bait should be recovered at a speed that suits the water. In a tumbling current, for instance, the minnow must be made to dart, else it will look like a bit of jetsam being swilled down-river. In quieter water a slower recovery is indicated. But not, as I said, too slow. Sea trout are used to minnows trying to escape and there-fore a sluggish bait must seem unnatural. An exception to this working theory is the drop-minnow, which will be dealt with in the next chapter.

The minnow-angler should have lots of tricks up his sleeve to add variety to the operations. The rod-tip may be jerked a little when recover-ing. This gives the minnow a very lively move-ment. Sea trout are frequently very cautious takers, however. They will stare at a minnow, follow it, and look at the thing from a dozen angles. If your minnow acts with the uncertain darting movements of the tiny fish it simulates then success is nearer than it is for the man who throws his bait and recovers it with a steady, unvarying wind. Aim to make your minnow act as it were really alive.

CHAPTER VI

DROP-MINNOW

THIS fascinating but little-practised way of catching sea trout is very deadly indeed if it is treated as the art it is. Let me give one illustration. A river had fallen in after a spate and many sea-trout anglers were busy with worm, fly and minnow. Presently an elderly man came down with a much-used rod which he kept ready set-up in his garden shed. In two hours he took a salmon and eight sea trout out of a reach that had been much fished-over. He did this by kneeling on the bank on a strip of oilskin and fishing a drop-minnow. Several of the other anglers left off fishing to watch. Artists are not all that common.

The drop-minnow is best fished in weed-free water, over gravel if possible, since it will repeatedly touch bottom. The bait is our old friend the preserved minnow in sizes 1½–2½ in. The tackles for the job (Fig. 11) may be made at home, although I think they are better bought since I am very awkward at the more fiddly jobs of tackle-making. A longish rod is needed for the method. The one I use is an old trout fly-rod, 10 ft. long, with the reel-fittings brought up the handle. In conjunction with this I use a 4-in. centre-pin reel of narrow diameter. The line is 4 lb. monofilament.

The whole essence of drop-minnowing is to

make the minnow behave like a small sick fish.
Sea trout normally chase and take live minnows
and therefore a sick minnow is unusual and
regarded with some suspicion. But the mere
fact that it makes no attempt to escape and acts
in such an expressive manner seems to excite
their predatory instincts. The only physical con-
trol you have over the minnow is of course
through the line and the leverage exerted by the
rod. Therefore it is no mean feat to make the
bait seem alive.

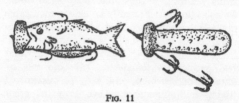

FIG. 11

TYPICAL DROP-MINNOW TACKLE

The first rule is to keep the drop-minnow in
the water as long as possible, provided it is
working effectively. Sea trout become mesmer-
ized by the antics of a drop-minnow and will
watch it for several minutes before making a
rush. These fish are probably not hungry. A
fly or a rapid-spinning devon would no doubt
fail to shift them. But the sight of a minnow
bobbing and wriggling in the stream seems to
operate some impulse in the fish's brain. Even
well-fed children will find room for an ice-cream !

The drop-minnow is cast from a centre-pin
reel by first stripping a few yards of line from the

reel and then casting the minnow with a gentle
underhand lobbing motion, releasing the spare
line as one does so. Once the minnow is in the
water let it sink to the bottom. When you know
it is down, impart some life by drawing in a few
inches of line with the left hand. If a current is
flowing this will be imparting life to the minnow
on its own account. Aim to keep the tiny bait
dipping and lifting a few inches above the stones
on the river-bed. Sea trout lurking under the
bank will be studying it carefully. Sooner or
later one will slide out and come to look closer
at the wobbling creature. If you see the gleam
of a fish do not think that more violent movements of the minnow will persuade it to take.
The suspicious brute will most likely sheer away
for good. Keep the minnow working at the same
tempo.

This method of catching sea-trout can be used
in high or low water if suitable variations are
employed. In high water a minnow of size
should be used. At such times I have successfully used the smallest size of silver sprat. On a
bright day with low water the angler needs to
pick his river-pitch with care. A steep bank with
deep water at the foot is excellent, especially if
there is a ripple of current. Get the minnow
beneath bushes and let it bob and work to its
heart's content. Provided the angler is fishing
down with the current it will do this for hours
if necessary.

Much of the success of the drop-minnow is
due to the fact that it gets down to the fish.
Skimming the surface with rapidly-recovered
artificials may be all very well when the fish are

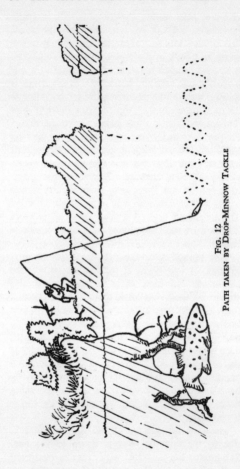

FIG. 12

PATH TAKEN BY DROP-MINNOW TACKLE

cruising and eager to take, but when they are lying deep under banks, amongst roots, the bait to stir them is one that hovers before their noses with tantalizing persistence.

LIVE-BAITING

By using a minnow-trap a supply of live minnows can be obtained for live-baiting. Few sea-trout anglers employ this method, mainly, I suppose, because they are unwilling to give it a serious trial. The main trouble is the minnow's extreme lightness, for unless a hair-like line is employed the weight of the line will drag the bait to the bottom. That is assuming that the minnow is on a free line, unencumbered by swivels or lead.

After several experiments I feel sure that the most effective way of showing sea trout a live minnow is to trot the bait downstream in the manner of grayling fishing. Rod, reel and line as for drop-minnowing may be used. The minnow should be near the river-bed and this may mean using a sliding-float. The minnow, of course, must travel slightly in advance of the float rather than vice versa. I assume a moder-ately-paced current.

RUNNING WORM

Many anglers, especially countrymen, rely on this method for taking their quota of sea trout. Considerable skill is needed and a mastery of the art of casting an almost weightless bait on a fine line. The method consists in presenting the worm so that it sinks and travels through the water in a perfectly natural way as though it has just been

washed into the river. No lead is used on the
line. The rod and 2-lb. line are the same as
described for drop-minnow fishing and the worm
is cast by the same lobbing motion.

The worm itself—which should be a toughened
brandling about 3 in. in length—is mounted on a
Pennell tackle. It is cast across and upstream,
always remembering that the best place to fish is
usually the white water at the throats of pools.
Keep the rod high so that as much line as possible
is in the air, thus reducing unnatural drag on the
bait. As the worm comes down and round,
recover line with the free hand to keep in touch
with it. One gives a gentle strike as soon as the
line stops, or if it begins to tremor.

When the water is high some anglers favour a
bunch of worms and fish them in the same way.
Lobs are often used and I fancy the sea trout
must mistake these writhing bunches for a shoal of
elvers, of which there are many in the summer river.

Running worm is frequently practised when
the water holds a tinge of colour. Provided the
angler takes great care not to be seen by the fish,
however, it is equally effective in clear water.
This often entails careful wading. Although there
is nothing wrong with wading when necessary,
I myself avoid it whenever possible. It is so
fatally easy to alarm sea trout by a clumsy step
and, unless I have no option, I prefer to take my
chance from the bank. In that case, kneeling
and crouching may be the needful tactics.

DAPPING AND CREEPER FISHING

Dapping with a live or an artificial fly is a
pretty method of catching sea trout at dusk in

high summer. Fish may be taken which are impossible to reach by other fishing methods. I have in mind a pool, very deep, bordered by a high bank thick with vegetation under which the fish lie. An inspection will reveal several gaps in the leafy wall wide enough to get a rod through. A soft-footed approach and a camp-stool for the dapper to sit on will allow him to practise his patient art for as long as need be.

I never use live insects for dapping—except for grasshoppers—partly because they are a nuisance to catch but also because they very soon become dead insects, no matter how carefully they are

FIG. 13
PENNELL WORMING TACKLE

mounted. An artificial Mayfly with trimmed wings makes a good dapping fly. Flies with furry bodies, resembling hover-flies, should be tried. Always remember to notice if caterpillars are active around the bushes where you are fishing. In summer they often suspend themselves down towards the water on suicidally long threads. If they are in evidence, an artificial caterpillar, if you have one, or a live one (tied lightly to the hook-shank with a bit of thread) may make a sea trout explode up from the depths. I have had a few goodly fish by dapping live wood-lice on the water surface. The lice are easily caught. They are lively creatures and presumably sea trout

take them for aquatic spiders. Grasshoppers
are excellent dapping baits, too.

A word about tackle. I like a short rod for
dapping and one that is fairly stiff. The one
I use was once a greenheart spinning rod and is
8 ft. 6 in. long. The line to use is monofil and
stout monofil at that—about 12 lb. is right. This
is comparatively hefty tackle, and so it must be
considering how little room you have for playing
your catch. In fact most fish will have to be kept
plunging on the top of the water until they are
tired out. To give them a foot of line will almost
certainly mean being hopelessly snagged in low
branches or tree-roots.

Dapping is especially interesting because you
can usually see the fish rise to the fly. It is a thrill
to see them do this although, admittedly, a large
proportion turn down again with a flick of their
tails. By using finer tackle you might hook these
fish but to land them is quite another matter.
Better to take a sporting chance with substantial
gear than deliberately invite breaks.

I mentioned that grasshoppers should be tried.
In fact they are one of the best summer baits and
I use them regularly during the season. The little
creatures are easy to catch if you set about it the
right way. Take a long-necked bottle, corked,
and go to a dry grassy meadow with a southern
aspect on a summer evening just when the heat is
going out of the day. The hoppers spring from
the grasses slow enough to be marked down and
caught. Later in the evening they disappear
under the grass-roots and are impossible to find.

Fig. 14 shows how to mount a hopper for
dapping. The top part of the thorax seems to

be the best place to enter the hook. Moreover, hooking them there leaves the hind legs free for a good kicking display—one of their main attractions. Sea trout will take hoppers fished underwater, too, but unfortunately the insects soon drown and a dead hopper is not of great value. I prefer the bright green variety of hopper; the bigger the better.

FIG. 14

GRASSHOPPER MOUNTED
FOR DAPPING

My experience of fishing with creepers (larvæ of the Stone Fly) is limited. The natural larvæ, or a suitable artificial, of which there are now some excellent ones, may be tried with profit. The natural creeper can be " worked " from a high bank, in the manner of a drop-minnow, while the artificials can be fished on the fly-line. Another natural bait that holds promise is the elver, say one about 3 in. long. Plenty of these are seen scaling waterfalls in the spring, and no doubt many a sea trout would show interest in such a bait.

WORM LEDGERING

This is a mighty dull way of killing a sporting fish but it is certainly effective and the method kills large numbers of sea trout each season.

The bait-bag should be stocked with a quantity of moss-scoured worms, as fat as you can obtain them. If you keep a garden " wormery," as many anglers do, an occasional dressing with oatmeal and diluted milk will render your worms fat and powerful.

For ledgering, take a rod of between 8 and 10 ft. in length and fit it with a reel—centre-pin or threadline—loaded with line of about 8 lb. breaking strain. Thread the line, then run a $\frac{1}{4}$ in. drilled bullet along it. Tie on a Pennell two-hook tackle. Nip a split shot to the line some three feet from the tackle and below the bullet. Then mount a nice active worm. (Fig. 15.)

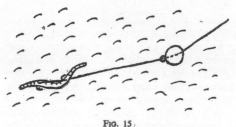

FIG. 15

WORM LEDGERING TACKLE

Ledgering may be practised in medium or high water. It is also good in low water at night. One chooses a fish-holding pool where underwater snags are not too numerous and casts the bait out in the normal way. Line is then slowly recovered until it is taut from bullet to rod-tip. The rod may be rested or laid on the grass. When a sea trout bites it will give the line a few vigorous plucks. These should be ignored. The fish will then either begin to run with the bait or the line will suddenly become slack, showing that the fish has moved the bullet over the bed in your direction. In both cases one should strike at once.

Apart from anything else the main snag about ledgering, to my mind, is the fact that many anglers—far too many—still use single hooks instead of two-hook Pennell tackles. The result is that they usually hook their sea trout deep down, small fish as well as big. Wee trout may fall victims; even smolts. Almost all these fish are so torn that it is a mercy to kill them. A two- or three-hook tackle, by making the bait more of a " mouthful," does tend to stay in the fish's mouth instead of being drawn at once into the gullet. In my view, single-hook worm fishing should be made illegal.

CHAPTER VII

ESTUARY FISHING

IN GENERAL

OF the several places where an angler may hopefully fish for sea trout, a river estuary is perhaps the most promising. Each season I spend much fishing time in learning just a little more about the ways of sea trout in estuaries. One of the first things one discovers is that very little has been published on the subject. One gathers that the estuary is usually neglected in favour of the river. I do not know why this should be; there are few better places for sea trout fishing.

Estuary fishing for sea trout is probably the best way of getting the sort of bag we all dream about. I have not had such a bag yet, although I have not done too badly. One point is that the fish from brackish water are beautifully fresh. Fresh water has not yet taken the sparkle from their bright bodies. Estuary sea trout are tigers when it comes to fighting it out, and there is ample water for them to make those rod-bending runs which so often end in a crashing leap which tests the tackle to its last ounce of strength. In Scotland the anglers esteem their estuary fishing and many do all their sea-trouting in brackish water. South of the border the estuary is so often neglected that I have even been asked, in a district noted for sea trout, what I was supposed to be doing fishing down there along the tidal channel! Anglers who decide to try their luck in an estuary must not be surprised if they find themselves to be pioneers.

PRELIMINARIES

Having decided to fish the estuary of the Z for sea trout, find out, first of all, exactly what sort of a place it is. There are mud estuaries and sand estuaries, and those which are a mixture of the two. Mud is no detriment provided it is safe to wade through, but sometimes it is deep, and deep mud is dangerous. Local people will always advise on such things. Sandy estuaries are the most comfortable ones to fish, although I prefer those with stony bottoms. The channels are more static in stone than in sand, and a close knowledge of the channel whereabouts is essential if success would crown your efforts. Moreover, sea trout will lie on stone and shingle. Mud, however, they find distasteful.

Most rivers which run sea trout are netted in the estuary by professional fishermen. It is well worth while spending an afternoon watching these people at work since a great deal can be learned from an examination of their catch. If asked nicely the netsmen will sell you a sea trout so that you can carry it away and perform an autopsy to discover its salt-water diet. Much of the stomach-contents will be jelly with a few staring eyes of unknown creatures. In the fish's gullet, however, may be a recently-swallowed morsel which can be identified. Possibly it is a baby sand-eel, a tiny crab or a small fish; or it may be a shrimp. Shrimps, prawns and other free-swimming creatures certainly provide the bulk of the sea trout's estuarine fare. Another food is

E

those marine crustaceans, the sea slaters, which may be seen on stone-work and old pilings at low water. They are not unlike wood-lice and love wet seaweed. Sand-hoppers are another diet item.

TACKLE

An essential tackle necessary for the estuary is a large net, minnow-mesh size or smaller, for the capture of shrimp bait. A shallow wooden box is needed, too, with plenty of holes in it and a hinged lid. A layer of damp seaweed in this will keep your supply of shrimps happy for several hours if it is not left in strong sunshine.

For spinning and drop-minnowing in estuaries I use a second-best rod liberally coated with varnish. It is an 8-ft. split-cane spinning-rod. This is also used for shrimp-fishing, although a rod a couple of feet longer would be better for the method. Monofilament in its 4-lb. size is the line to use, for whatever method, and the reels are both threadline and centre-pin (for shrimp-fishing). A supply of the tough preserved minnows should also be in the bag although if there were rock pools in the estuary I should prefer to net a few of the small fish which thrive in them and use these in preference to minnows. With these simple tackle variations the angler is quite prepared for estuary work. A thick sweater, a duffle-coat and gum boots will afford him ample protection in all but the worst weather.

SHRIMP FISHING

I have given some thought to the question of how to make a shrimp behave naturally in tidal water, and there seems only one solution to the problem. The shrimp must be alive and able to move freely and it must be fished on a tackle that will present it effectively to the fish. Before describing this tackle I will say a word about the bait itself. The shrimps to use should be well-developed specimens of about 1½ in. in length, bigger if you can get them, but not above 2 in. A net of ¼-in. square mesh will select the right ones and let the small stuff through. Having put the shrimps under their eiderdown of damp sea-weed in the box we can tackle-up.

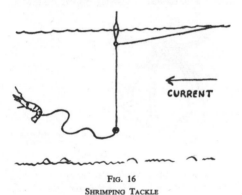

FIG. 16

SHRIMPING TACKLE

The whole idea behind this method of fishing is to present a live shrimp to the sea trout in such a manner that the crustacean is indistinguishable from its brethren. I have found only one way of doing this satisfactorily, and Fig 16 makes the lay-out plain. A float, a small drilled bullet and a size 8 fly-hook are used. I prefer good quality fly-hooks rather than "sea-hooks" because the wire is fine and they are always perfectly tempered. The best sort of float I find to be a 4-in. cork-bodied roach float with a fluorescent tip. This is of the sliding type, or is easily made so.

Now to mount tackle and bait. The float is threaded on the line by its bottom ring and run up out of the way. Then the drilled bullet is threaded. Finally the hook is tied on, using one of the well-known nylon knots such as the one illustrated (Fig. 17). Next take a medium-sized split shot and nip it to the line, three feet or so from the hook and below the bullet. Allow the

FIG. 17

A USEFUL KNOT FOR
SECURING HOOKS

float to slide down while you tie into the line a bit of rubber band. This is the float-stop and the distance between this and the hook varies, of course, according to the fishing depth required. Much estuary fishing is done at a depth of between 10 and 15 feet, so it follows that a sliding float is the best device for the job. In shallow water the float may be fixed in the usual way.

The shrimp should be put on the hook with some care. Avoid crushing it with your fingers whilst removing it from the box. Enter the hook in the third segment from the tail-end by means of a shallow skin-hold. Anglers who are skilled at mounting gentles on hooks will know exactly what I mean. By hooking it thus the shrimp will not only survive longer but will work better (Fig. 18).

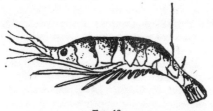

FIG. 18
THE SHRIMP

In fishing, the tackle is lowered into the channel, whereupon the bullet will cock the float by bringing the line-stop down to it. The current will then begin to drift the tackle. The angler now has three main concerns—to give line (or walk along the shore) as the float advances; to retard the float a little from time to time, thus ensuring that the shrimp is fishing in advance of the line; and to manœuvre the float, by whatever method seems best, into all likely water. The effect of all this is easy to imagine. The shrimp, which is lightly tethered to three feet of free line, will be giving an excellent performance of jerking and swimming, in the manner of the species. It should be fishing not more than a yard or two from the bottom, since incoming shoals of sea trout invariably swim deep, the better to dodge porpoise. However, if the day is dark or the water much stained by sand, it may be advisable to fish the shrimp in mid-water.

Quite often it is possible to fish the estuary for long distances without taking the tackle from the water. One simply walks along the shore keeping the rod high so that the line is in the air and not on the water, collecting rubbish. A bite is indicated by the instantaneous disappearance of the float. I have never found it necessary to strike quickly at sea trout taking a shrimp. The luscious mouthful seems so innocent that it is browsed and the fish moves away, oblivious of being connected with an angler. A gentle but resolute tightening of the line usually serves to plant the hook and disillusion the fish. Sometimes the angler may find that his strike misses. Sea trout will nip the torso off a shrimp with great precision, leaving the tail on the hook. This is the reason why the bait should not be over-large. The single hook will fail to cover it.

Other fish than sea trout will take a shrimp fished thus in an estuary. Bass in particular are very partial to shrimp. Yet I find that bass and sea trout seldom mix. At low water, for instance, bass are rare whilst sea trout may be abundant—and I personally prefer to fish a shrimp when the water is low.

This question of tide-state is of some importance. The fresh water condition of the river is important too, since a spate will bring sea trout shoaling into the estuary. Many sea anglers like to fish on a rising tide. But, for sea trout, I prefer low water. One reason is that the river-channel is clearly visible—and sea trout always run the channel. A second reason is that there is less trouble from drifting weed. Moreover, shrimp-fishing is better practised in a light current than in the swirling torrents of ebb and flow. This is of particular importance in mud or soft sand estuaries since the run of tide soon makes them unfishable, the water becoming like porridge. Sea trout dislike filth and go elsewhere. All good reasons for glancing at a tide-table and choosing a time for fishing when the stream runs quiet and clean in its salty gully.

In some estuaries weed is a great problem. In extreme cases it will make fishing impossible. There is nothing more infuriating than to find the water full of hair-like green strands when all other factors indicate a successful outing. The only way I have found of minimizing this trouble is to fish the shrimp down with the current on a nylon paternoster tied to the line. A $\frac{1}{2}$-oz. drilled bullet, or suitable lead, gives the line bottom anchorage. The monofilament paternoster, mounted with a No. 8 hook, is tied three feet or so above the lead. No float is used. After mounting the shrimp, the outfit is lowered into a tidal gully of good depth where sea trout are likely to be lying. A tight line is kept between lead and rod-tip. This method reduces the amount of line in the water, thus minimizing weed-collection. It makes fishing in weedy water possible, if not comfortable (Fig. 19).

When the sea begins to run into the river-mouth the sea trout usually go off feed. No doubt most of them start working upstream. And although fresh runs of fish are coming over the bar they are

mostly too busy travelling to pause over a shrimp.
For such conditions, spinning is probably the best
treatment.

SPINNING IN ESTUARIES

Many lures, good and otherwise, may be col-
lected in the tackle-bag for estuary spinning.
Imitation sand-eels, plastic ragworms, tube baits
and a galaxy of flashing devices, from mackerel-
spinners to devons, are at the angler's command.
A bait I have not tried yet, but which might well
prove deadly, is a lip-hooked elver spun very
slowly through the channels.

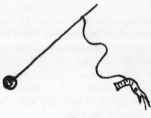

FIG. 19
SIMPLE PATERNOSTER FOR
WEEDY ESTUARIES

If the tide is high I think there is little to beat
a good spoon, provided it is the right type and
weight. In the chapter on tackle maintenance I
describe how such spoons can be made. For
estuary work a spoon should be slim and of the
right shape, or else it does not " work " properly
(Fig. 20). Such spoons do not revolve, they
flicker through the water, which is more natural

and fetching than a violent turning over and over.
For sea trout, spoons should be about 2½ in. long
and ¾ in. wide. The shape is the shape of a
willow-leaf. This shape and size, I fancy, does
approximate to the sea trout's main diet item
whilst at sea—the young herring.

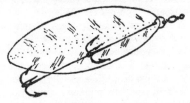

FIG. 20
SEA TROUT SPOON

Any of the other lures may be tried experi-
mentally, not forgetting the preserved minnow if
the water is clear enough to use it with hope. If
a suitable shrimp spinning-mount is in the bag a
shrimp can be mounted, too, and run over the
likely spots.

FLY-FISHING

I have never fished a fly in an estuary, the chief
reason being that I shrink from impregnating my
fly-line and reel with salt, than which there is no
worse spoiler of tackle. Yet if sport promised to
be brisk enough I should probably throw caution
to the winds. In some river estuaries anglers
catch many sea trout on fly. Thus there is nothing
novel about the method, and if sea trout are rising
it is certainly worth serious trial. Flies may be
had which resemble shrimps and other sea-
creatures, and some of these might be usefully

tried along with more conventional patterns. From observation, I find that sea trout rise freely in the first sea-pool of the river, at the junction between salt and fresh water.

WHERE TO FISH IN ESTUARIES

In most rivers there is a place where the water quietens as it approaches the level of the salt. It usually attains its last few feet of fall to true sea-level by means of a run or stickle. I have always found such places very good at low water for sea trout. The fish love to lie in the brisk stream until the next tide and will take spun baits with a dash, especially minnows, natural or quill, and small devons.

For shrimp-fishing, the angler gets a little nearer to the sea, to where the deeply-etched channel flows quiet and mysterious. I have one estuary in mind that fishes very well from just behind the bar. The broad stream closes in to a cut between high sandy walls, and from there to the bar the bed is stony and the water some 8 to 10 ft. deep. Plenty of sea trout and a few salmon are found there at low water. Significantly enough it is a favourite place for the netsmen to unfurl their long seines and several thousand pounds' weight of fine sea trout are taken therefrom each season. At week-ends the nets do not operate and this is when I arrange to be at hand with a rod and abundant hope. The angler who is interested in this branch of sea trouting should spend some time in quietly seeking out such places, for there he will do much satisfying execution.

CHAPTER VIII

PLAYING AND GRASSING

STRIKING SEA TROUT

EACH season many sea trout are lost because anglers forget, in the urgency of the moment, to twitch the hook home. This is especially so whilst spinning since the fish seize the bait so vigorously that they partially hook themselves. Sometimes they make a job of it and the angler is firmly connected. Quite often however, the hook is merely lodged, possibly between the teeth or on a bony angle of the jaw. A swift twist and jump by the fish soon gets rid of the tackle. Therefore it is good sense and good practise to hit the fish with a quick flick of the rod as soon as you know it is on. To delay, even for a second, may mean a sad parting. Unless the hook is firmly embedded below the barb the chances of landing a fresh sea trout are small.

THE FIRST TWO MINUTES

After a sea trout is hooked the odds are that it will strip some line from the reel and indulge in several leaps. The angler must strike his fish before it starts leaping since this puts a great strain on the tackle and a loosely-connected hook will soon throw adrift. The fish jumps and the angler lets it have its will, for nothing blunts the edge of a sea trout's energy quicker.

While this is going on one should be assessing the size of the fish and deciding which is the best position from which to play it. The bank-fisher may have trees and bushes to contend with. The wading angler will have to watch the fish and at the same time keep his precarious footing. The main rule in playing a sea trout is to keep it working upstream. If the fish takes fright and flashes down with the current then the angler must get below it and quickly, if it is a big one. Otherwise several pounds of effective weight will have been added to the fish, depending on how strong the water is running. Apart from anything else, this extra weight may well tear the hook from its hold or it may break the line. With big sea trout, therefore, get below at all costs—even if this means slackening off the line and passing the rod round the bases of bankside trees.

This raises another point—on whether sea trout should or should not be played on a tight line. Keeping the line tight is almost a fetish with some anglers, I do not know why. In my view it is good practice to give the fish a completely slack line on occasion. For example, if a sea trout seems determined to rush out of the pool—and the angler is unable to follow—a slack line often meets the emergency. Tightening up will, in any case, only make the fish more determined to be gone. A sudden slackening of tension, however, often makes the fish hesitate, particularly if the water is low and it is reluctant to leave the safety of the pool. Brute tactics have no place in modern sea trout fishing, whether the lure is fly or bait. When a fish cannot be outwitted it can usually be coaxed.

After the first two minutes the angler will know

several things. He should have a good idea of what size of a fish he is dealing with. Having struck it, he is reasonably sure that the hook is well home. If the fish has been springing about it will now have settled down to a hard running battle that can only end in escape or capture. The angler will also have spotted a likely place to beach the fish or a backwater to gaff it, if he is using a gaff. By altering his position on the bank or in the water he will have ensured that the sea trout is upstream of him.

TIRING A FISH

The best way of tiring a fish is to make it leap, and sea trout do this of their own accord. Another way is to induce the fish to enter a fast current. Five minutes in a strong run of water will tire even a very big sea trout, especially if the angler is applying lateral pressure. Such fish will often take the bit between their teeth and try to forge upstream to the next pool. A few minutes of this hectic stuff and they are ready for grassing.

" Pumping " is another device for weakening strong fish. The rod-point is lowered, the line wound up hard, then the rod is slowly raised. The spring effect of the rod takes the weight of of the fish. This is repeated as often as necessary until the sea trout is near enough to gaff. If the fish decides to run, then the angler lets it. When it stops, he resumes pumping.

I mentioned lateral pressure above. This is a method of pulling on a fish to the best advantage. Really, it is a question of leverage. A big sea trout is able to withstand a strong direct pull from a rod, provided it is not pulled off-balance (see Fig. 21). Lateral pressure is intended to throw the fish off-balance, and that is why it is so effective. By pulling at right-angles to the sea trout's body-line the effect of the pull is much increased. It is hardly necessary to add that the whole effect of these tactics is to kill the sea trout as quickly and cleanly as possible.

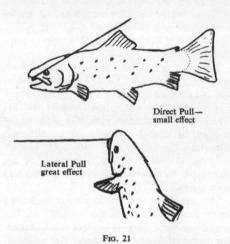

Direct Pull—
small effect

Lateral Pull
great effect

FIG. 21

EFFECT OF LATERAL PULL WHEN PLAYING FISH

GRASSING

Many anglers are clumsy with a gaff, possibly because they use one but seldom and the event makes them nervous over losing a fish for which they have worked hard. Ensure first that the sea trout is quite spent. The first sign of this is when it begins to float on top of the water. After a final thresh around it will turn on its side. The gaff should then be laid across its tail, level with the vent, and be drawn home in one smooth stroke, the fish then being lifted clear of the water (Fig. 22). Fish should always be taken well back from the river before attempt is made to kill them and remove the hook, otherwise they will struggle and may get away after breaking the line.

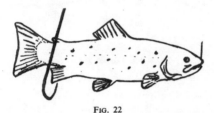

FIG. 22
SEA TROUT IN POSITION FOR GAFFING

Beaching a fish on a shingle beach is safe and simple. By standing well back from the water and pulling when the fish wriggles the angler may draw it on to dry land. Another method is to tail it by hand. Rub the hand in the nearest grit and grasp the sea trout by the " wrist ", thumb to the rear, whilst holding its head high with the rod. It may then he half-lifted, half-carried ashore (Fig. 23).

Sea trout are readily killed by a hard blow over the head. I use the handle of my small gaff for this job. I also carry a small pike-gag to help in the removal of hooks. Big sea trout have vicious teeth and the gag has proved its worth on many occasions. Having once been bitten by an 8-lb. cock fish I prefer to play it safe.

FIG. 23

GRASP FOR TAILING A SEA TROUT

CHAPTER IX

TACKLE MAINTENANCE

IN GENERAL

SOME sea trout tackle can be made easily; and some cannot. Rods, I think, are better bought, even if they are only second-hand. Rod-making is a highly-skilled craft and, quite frankly, I think few amateurs can hope to do it successfully. For one thing, they have not the specialized machinery of the firms; and, for another, they have not the wide day-to-day experience. This personal view is sharpened by the fact that I have seen several sea-trouters with home-made rods which were quite unsuitable. Having got a decent rod, no matter how old, look after it. And that means a thin coat of varnish each season and a close check of all rings and tyings in search of any broken or frayed. Rings of the agate-lined type have a wicked habit of developing hair-like cracks which wear the line at a furious rate. For this reason I prefer plain, stainless steel rings. They are light and cheap.

Reels are often given a pat and a polish and expected to perform their important functions without further ado. Although the manufacturers fit devices for quick dismantling many reels are never taken apart in months. This despite the fact that they are subjected to grit, sand, salt and much besides. Threadline reels should be lubricated according to makers' instructions, which may mean putting a spot of oil in half a dozen places. All reels need to be cleaned and oiled after returning from fishing. I do this with mine as a matter of course, not so that I can feel virtuous, but because a squeaky, grating reel wears away good money, besides being a distraction.

Some meticulous anglers oil their fly-hooks and the metal parts of bait-tackles as a rust preventative. My patience does not run to this, but I do keep such hooks in a box on dry cotton wool, which absorbs much of the moisture. After estuary fishing everything you use must be sluiced in fresh water, otherwise it will very soon become rotten. Minnow and other tackles should be held under a tap then hung to dry. Otherwise they very soon become unreliable and such things as hook-barbs fracturing occur with mysterious regularity.

SPOON MAKING

The sea trout angler, no matter how expert, needs a good stock of baits to start off the season. Ideally, this stock should be kept up. On a bad day I expect to lose three baits or tackles. This is unavoidable and a part of the game. Sunken trees and what-not take their toll and there is little that can be done about it except cut the cost of baits to a minimum.

I make my spoons out of discarded motorcycle headlamp rims. The brass is of the right gauge and the chromium gives the lure a nice flash. The rim is first cut in half with tinsnips, then it is roughly flattened out. A cardboard "template" and a pencil serves to outline the spoon-shape, which is then cut out with the snips. Discreet tapping with a hide hammer and bending with pliers will adjust the curvature of the spoon. A $\frac{1}{8}$ in. hole is drilled at one end and a split-ring entered fitted with a swivel. The hook link can be made of wire or nylon. I like it flexible, to minimize leverage by the fish. That is all there is to it.

SUNDRIES

The sea trout angler must be mobile if he is to get the best out of his sport. That means having a capacious carrier which will hold everything needed for a day's outing. I do not use a creel but prefer a stout canvas side-bag with a webbing sling. One with two compartments is best; fish at the back, tackle and lunch at the front. I carry a 3-ft. square of oilskin salvaged from a discarded raincoat in which I roll my sea trout. The material is easily washed and it saves making the bag smelly. In the bag is a pair of long-nosed pliers, scissors, and a hank of thick string. A canvas loop, sewn in by myself, holds a thermos in place.

Waders are another item that can cause much bother if neglected. Ordinary thigh waders meet the needs of most anglers; in fact many use only gum-boots. I once hesitated over buying a pair of trouser waders and then realized how hot the things would be on a sunny day if one needed to walk a lot between pools. Meantime, I carry on with thigh waders, and the main trouble I meet is have the things punctured by blackthorns. The only answer to this is to cover the hole with one of those patches which are sold with a metallic protective skin. Once in position they never budge. Damp does not hurt waders; but sweat does. A dry newspaper, thrust inside each wader after fishing, keeps them dry and sweet. A new pair of waders usually lasts me through three seasons.

CASTS AND LINES

The use of monofilament for casts, traces and spinning lines saves the angler from much of the fuss that was attendant on previous materials. But if it is neglected and forgotten it will give trouble, which means, in most cases, a lost fish.

Every season I use two 100-yard lengths of 4-lb. monofilament for spinning. The first line is put on at the opening of the season and is discarded in July. The other is used from July to September. After a few weeks use with each line I reverse it so that the outer portion is wound on the drum first. Before fishing, I check the last ten yards or so for flaws or excessive wear. The lines are usually left on the reel, wet, a lazy practice I do not defend. However, my precautions seem adequate, since I am seldom broken by fish except for reasons that have nothing to do with the line.

The life and strength of monofilament is extended by observing small rules. It should always be cut; never broken by pulling, otherwise the adjacent portions are stretched and weakened. The same applies when a bait or fly is caught up in an obstruction. If the lure is recovered by more or less violent tugging the cast should be discarded. The elasticity of monofilament has a definite limit and once you exceed it, even momentarily, it becomes unreliable.

Plaited silk fly-lines are easily kept in good

order by rubbing them with a soft cloth and applying a little wax furniture polish. As regards floatants, both for line and flies, I like very much the types containing silicones.

STORING TACKLE

The angler's sea trout tackle will be laid away from early October until April. If it is stored with care it will survive the winter without serious deterioration. If it is bundled away then spring will reveal a pretty wreck.

I hang my rods on hooks, flaps and tapes loose, in the corner of a dry bedroom. Reels should be cleaned and oiled and put away in a cupboard safe from small experimental fingers.

As regards minnow and other small tackles, I am almost bound to recommend discarding used ones at the end of the season. I always discard mine, mainly because the tiny trebles and swivels are almost certain to have become touched with rust at some time and a few months inactivity renders them unreliable for the harsh test of sea trouting. The leads may be retained, however, and the angler may tie on new trebles if he can work happily with such small items.

I carefully check over my flies on some autumn night, touching the hooks with an oil-stone, and adding a bit of silk to frayed bodies. Then I give the hooks a touch with an oily rag and lay the flies in a box with cotton wool at the bottom.

Monofilament casts should be wrapped on cardboard holders and lines are best run off reels and wound loosely on to wooden bobbins. Silk fly-lines should be looped into a large figure-of-eight, tied in the middle with cotton, and hung near the rods. Commonsense care, all of this, but what a difference it makes when you come to plan the season's first trip and know everything is in perfect order.

SUMMING UP

In this book I have tried to present sea trout angling as a wonderful sport that is open to everyone. It is true that everyone does not live within a few yards of sea trout water like I do, yet the speedy coach can take anglers to distant places in a short time. It seems a good idea, therefore, to offer suggestions to anglers who may want to go sea trout fishing in a group. I urge that a member of the group makes a personal visit first and obtains definite permission both for the parking of the coach and for bringing a party of his fellows fishing. This commonsense precaution can save all sorts of unpleasantness and will lay the foundations for your welcome on subsequent visits. Coach parties, I suggest, should choose a nice sandy estuary served by a sea trout river. The best months are from June to September, always avoiding times of severe drought.

The sea trout is a gypsy of a fish, here today, gone tomorrow. A bright ¾-lb. whitling may snatch the lure almost anywhere. I have had them in 3-foot-wide brooks when, by every rule of the book, they should have been at sea. You may see them springing perkily over the waves of the estuary tide at almost any time of the year. The whitling, or young sea trout, is like Peter Pan—it never grows up; for, as one matures and ages and dies, another comes to fill its place. In that small shining body springing so jauntily at the waterfall is symbolized all that is best in the angler's world—the optimism, the never-failing interest, and the freedom.

Yet freedom can only be comparative and no living thing is utterly free—certainly not the human angler. Freedom—particularly of the river bank—must be paid for by respect for other people's interests. Which raises the question of litter and those who leave it behind. No true angler leaves litter. The damage is done by fools who can't or won't see how fast they are closing sea trout and other water to themselves and others. These so-called fishermen are fashioning chains for their own ankles and when every water is labelled " Strictly Private " perhaps they will be satisfied. But I fancy that the sound common-sense and discipline of the angling fraternity at large will stop the rot in time. In some places it has already been stopped.

In a small book there is no room for personal stories, no space to describe a particular shady pool which always holds fish, nor time to enthuse for a few pages on the real and vivid beauty of the countryside early on a summer morning when the river flows swift and clean over its gravels and all is peace. The reader must take all this for granted and seek for himself. Somewhere there is a pool which he can call his own, even if only in his own mind. Somewhere there swims a sea trout—or the father of a sea trout—which will be the first he has ever grassed. All this in the future, waiting to be taken and savoured. I only hope I have shown the way with sufficient clearness.

Angling, I think, is not so much a sport as a way of life. The angler's mind becomes directed outwards at the shifting facets of nature's scene instead of dwelling on his own troubles. If it is a contemplative recreation then the contemplation is wholly healthy. And with sea trout angling a life-time is scant enough time to understand the tale that goes on, year in and year out, beneath the river-water. There is always something new to record. Sea trout obey their own laws and no one, I think, will understand these in their entirety, although it is a pleasure to try.

There are still a few points to draw together and one of these is river-bank courtesy. When several anglers are fishing a river certain rules of conduct must be observed, and the chief of these is to let the other chap have complete possession of the pool he is fishing. Anglers have often cut in above or below me and fished water that I was preparing to fish myself. When it is a case of bad manners, not ignorance, I swear forcibly in the best R.A.F. tradition and tell them to get to hell out. When the boot is on the other foot and I arrive late I expect to fish vacant water, or wait my turn for a pool.

It is surprising, too, how often one's fishing is spoiled by the thoughtless movements of anglers arriving or departing. A man who will spend all afternoon crawling on his belly to throw lures over shy fish will finally stand up, pack his rod, and go whistling along the bank with heavy foot-falls. Luckless anglers still fishing may as well pack up too.

The present outlook for sea trout angling is hopeful. The River Boards of to-day are showing imagination and foresight. Sea trout ova have been planted in rivers that were made barren by

mine and other pollutions. Experiments have
been made with artificial redds and observation
chambers cut into river banks. Sea trout smolts
have been pond-reared to a sturdy size, and then
released in thousands into suitable river systems.
And, as I noted earlier, serious attempts are being
made to bring the sea trout back to East Anglia
and South-East England. This worthy work must
go on. For the sea trout may be called the river's
conscience; it delights in complete cleanliness.
And when filth sullies our waterways—even if
only in small quantities—the sea trout goes elsewhere. His absence is a reproof and a challenge.

APPENDIX

It seems probable that fewer British anglers fish for sea trout than for any other single species. They have received only a meagre share of the publicity accorded salmon, brown trout and the coarse fishes, and in consequence many anglers never think of them even when they are fishing sea-trout waters.

Anyone who follows the excellent instructions in the foregoing pages can go out and catch sea trout—subject to the vagaries that affect all forms of angling. Mr. Holiday has also given these fish that measure of praise they so well deserve, and to reinforce his comments I repeat below a few short opinions on sea trout expressed by angling writers over four centuries.

GENERAL EDITOR

" And this may be believed of the Fordige Trout, which, as it is said of the stork, that he knows his season, so he knows his times, I think almost his day of coming into that river out of the sea; where he lives, and, it is like, feeds, nine months of the year, and fasts three in the river of Fordidge. And you are to note, that these townsmen are very punctual in observing the time of beginning to fish for them; and boast much, that their river affords a Trout that exceeds all others."—IZAAK WALTON, *The Compleat Angler*, 1653.

" The Fordich Trout, which is so much talked

of, seems to be of a different sort from the rest, because it is almost as big as a Salmon, and lives nine months in the sea."—RICHARD BROOKES, *The Art of Angling*, 1740.

" In fly-fishing for large white trout (*Sewin*) in Ireland, the angler should use very strong gut for the bottom, for the trout are very strong and yield noble sport, and may be known on being hooked; they immediately leap out of the water."—G. A. HANSARD, *Trout and Salmon Fishing*, 1834.

" There is no fish that I know of which affords, on being hooked, such sport to the angler. In proportion to their size, they are much stronger and more wayward in their movements than the salmon, and test to a greater extent the sufficiency of the tackle."—THOMAS TOD STODDART, *The Angler's Companion*, 1847.

" The white trout is one of the gamest fish that swims. Like a champion of the light-weights he is all activity: when hooked he is here, there, and everywhere, now up, now down, now in the water and now out."—FRANCIS FRANCIS, *A Book on Angling*, 1867.

" In the north the sea trout is equally abundant with the salmon, and large quantities find their way to the southern towns, where they are retailed by the fish dealers, whose boisterous cry of 'Salmon without any gammon!' is heard whenever a fresh instalment arrives. In many cases these people have been unwittingly 'gammoned' themselves, their customers, nevertheless, being the ultimate dupes. From the fisherman's point of view, the sea trout is equal to the finest grilse that ever ascended Tay or Tweed, exceeding, as he does, for gameness and pertinacity every other British fish."—DAVID FOSTER, *The Scientific Angler*, 1882.

" I prefer a good fresh run sea trout of three or four pounds in a river on a single-handed rod and fine tackle to anything else."—LORD GREY, *Fly Fishing*, 1899.

> " The wildest, the best,
>   And the bravest of fishes
> And, however he's dressed,
>   The most dainty of dishes."
>   PATRICK CHALMERS

INDEX